Shires
"The great Horse"
For Kids

Nature Books for Kids
By
K. Bennett

Mendon Cottage Books

JD-Biz Publishing

Read More Amazing Animal Books

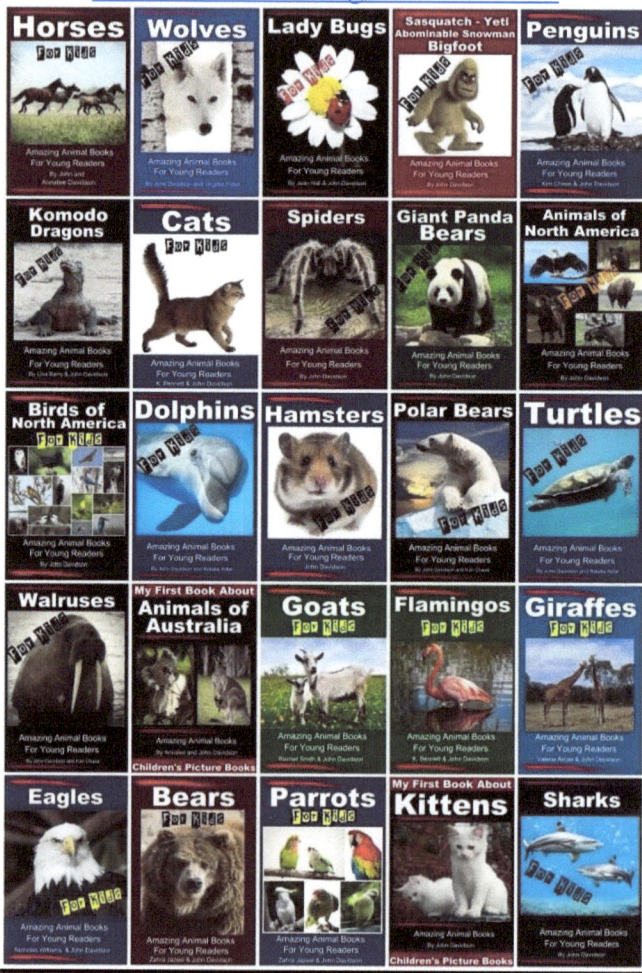

Purchase at Amazon.com

Shire

Table of Contents

Introduction

Shire

Introduction

"THE HIGH HORSE"
By Carolyn Wells

The High Horse often takes a foremost place
Among the winners of the human race.
They say one needs both brawn and brain to ride him,
And even then 'tis very hard to guide him.
His jockeys gaily prance and boldly scoff,
But soon or late they're sure to tumble off.

***

Shire: Shires are called the "gentle giants" of the horse world. They are calm, patient, loving and willing to serve. These horses are part of the "draught" or "draft" horse breed. Do you remember what a "draft" horse is?

A draft horse.

This is a horse that "draws" or "hauls" something. It is also called a work horse or heavy horse, because it works hard and pulls heavy loads. However, these types of horses are strong, docile, easy to work with and very patient. Do you know why?

Shire

Imagine if these tall, strong horses were hard to handle. It would be dangerous to be around them, and riding them could be risky! Happily, Shires are not like that. They are gentle and kind despite their large size.

How big are they?

Shires are very big and stand very tall. Called the tallest of the horse breeds, some Shires are 19 hands tall.

Where do Shires come from?

Shires come from English horses known as the "Old English Black horse." In the past, Shires pulled heavy carts full of ale. (Ale: *is a drink made from malt. It is bitterer than beer – Dictionary.com*). They also hauled farming equipment and cleared heavy marshland. Shires also carried Knights into battle wearing full body armor.

Shires were very important to the economy of England. *Cotebrookshirehorses.co.uk* says there were millions of these beautiful horses at one time. Remember: there were no paved roads in those days or highways. So people needed really strong horses to pull heavy loads.

After many years of hard labor, Shires became a part of Royal processions where they got a new name: **Drum horses**. Can you guess why? It is because the riders were drummers and played the drums.

What makes this horse special?

Today, Shires are used in forestry, fun driving, advertising and events. With their loving personality, gentle nature and big heart, Shires are great horses and interesting to learn about!

Shire

HOW TO DRAW A SIMPLE HORSE FOR KIDS:

Would you like to learn how to draw a horse? Wikihow.com has a simple, but neat tutorial. Here are the steps to get started:

1- First, ask your parent's or a guardian's permission to go online.

2- In your browser (Chrome, Internet explorer, Firefox, Torch) type: www.Wikihow.com

3- In the search box at the top of the page type: *Draw a simple horse.* Once the search is complete, you should see a title that reads: **"How to draw a simple horse: 11 steps with pictures**."

4 – Click on the link and follow the steps.

5- Have fun!

Shire

Chapter 1

Hello there!

History: To understand where this noble breed came from, we have to go back in time to the 16th century. In those years, Dutch engineers came to England to do some work. And when they got to England they came with their horses called Friesian.

After many years passed by, another type of horse came from Friesian horses. These were called *Old English Black Horse.* Some people tried to improve this horse and soon another horse appeared called the "Bakewell Black."

Two horses descended from the Bakewell Black. One was the Fen or Lincolnshire and the other was called: Leicester or Midlands's type.

What made these horses unique?

Shire

Fen type horse: These horses were larger, have extra hair and more bone.

Midlands type: Stronger, more endurance and look cuter!

During the middle part of the 17th century, the term "Shire horse" was used. But it would take many more years until the end of the 18th century, where we meet a horse called the "Packington Blind Horse."

This Stallion is where Shires come from.

How were Shires used?

People used Shires to pull their cart and move their goods from one place to another. Shires were also used to help farmers plough. Do you remember what this word means?

Plough: A farmer plants different things. And he has to get the seeds into the ground and cover them with enough dirt to grow; so a plough is a handy instrument to use.

Did you ever try to plant something with just your hands? Is it easy or hard to do? This is one reason why farmers use a plough. It makes their job a lot easier!

Today, Shires are considered "critical." Why?

According to the American Livestock Breeds Conservancy, the amount of Shires in the world is less than 2,000.

The Equus Survival trust organization says there are between 500 to 1500 active mares.

But there is good news!

Shirehorse.org says today, in the year 2015, there are about 3,000 Shires in the world! This means many people are doing their best to save this amazing animal.

Shire

FUN FACTS FOR KIDS: What is HANDS?

This is a neat way to measure horses. The measurement refers to hands, literal hands!

Many years ago, people did not have rulers or measuring sticks like we do today. So they used whatever they had…and they had hands. So horses are measured in hands. You can do this too! One hand is 4 inches.

So if a horse is 15 hands multiply this by 4. (15 x 4) and you will get 60 inches. And if a horse is 16 hands multiply this number by 4. (16 x 4) and you will get 64 inches.

Now that you know how to do it, you can measure the other horses for yourself. Have fun!

Do you like my beautiful coat?

Strengths: Shires are usually easy to work with and they work hard. They are eager to please and willing to learn what you teach them. This does not mean all Shires are alike. Some may be a little cranky but most Shires are patient and easygoing.

A good thing about Shires is how brave they are. They do not spook quickly. So if something pops up and goes BOO, your Shire will not run away looking for somewhere to hide! It would have to be something much bigger to scare them.

An example of this is how Shires were used in big cities to pull omnibuses. ***Animals.Pawnnation.com*** says, "Not much surprises them!"

Out for a trot

Weaknesses: You already know there are not many of these beautiful animals left. So if you wanted to get one, it might be a little hard to find the "right" one.

It would also be expensive to feed. Do you know how much a Shire can weigh? Look under "Characteristics" and you will see the answer! Now imagine how much food it would take to feed an animal this size.

Shires also get sick especially in their legs. This disease causes leg spasms and because of the feathering, they can suffer from infection.

(**Source:** Jane Meggitt, Demand Media)

CURIOUS FACT FOR KIDS:

Duke is a beautiful Shire and he is very tall. In 2008, he was measured at 19 hands, but an article on Telegraph.co.uk dated May 26, 2009 measured him at 20.1 hands tall. Do you remember how to calculate the inches? Is Duke a lot taller than you? How much taller?

The article also says he weighs as much as a family car. But guess what? He's afraid of mice. Poor Duke!

Pulling together

Characteristics: As we talked about in the beginning, Shires are big horses and very tall.

Height: Mares stand approximately 16 hands and over. Stallions stand at approximately 17 hands and over.

Weight: 2,000 - 3,000 pounds and up.

Shires have beautiful coat colors like bay, black or grey. White is also a beautiful color and Roan. Have you ever heard of this color before?

Shire

Roan: This is not just one color. It is a pattern of colors with a mixture of white. The horse will have lots of white hairs mixed with their other hairs. Usually the head, lower legs, mane and tail are more solid or will have fewer white hairs. Sometimes, this color variation is called Silvery.

Now, look at a Shires feet. Do you see anything different? You will probably see feathering on their ***fetlocks***. If you've never heard of this word before it simply means: Ankle. No, this is not the correct term, but it is a word we can easily understand. Do you have any feathers on your ankles?

Look at my socks!

Shire Training: These horses are highly intelligent and easy to train. Their docile nature and obedience makes it not only fun for the owner but also for the horse!

What's the best way to train a Shire? An online article written by **_Kay Baxter at Ehow.co.uk_** recommends the following ways to train them:

1- Feeding your horse daily with good hay and feed (pelleted) is a great way to start. Don't you work and learn better after you eat? Your horse will too!

2- Clean water is very important, so make sure your horse has enough to drink. And it will keep them well hydrated and feeling good inside.

3-Groom and brush the horses' coat every day. And keep the hoofs clean. Sometimes rocks and dirt can get stuck inside, so it's nice to take it out. Imagine how happy your horse will feel after it has clean shoes!

4- Work with Shires when they are young. Teach them to stand still when they are tied. Teach them to obey when you lead them. Teach them to be still when bathing and trimming them. If you teach them when they are young, then when they get older it will not be that difficult.

Regular Training: There is more to training Shires than just these points. **_EagleRidgeSuffolk.com_** recommends respecting the horse's wishes and getting them to trust you. It also involves getting the horse to want to spend time with you.

There are several ways to do this and **_Wikihow_** recommends the following steps:

1-**_First of all, don't scare the horse_**. That means you should not run up or sneak up on them suddenly. This is not a hard to understand. For example, do you like it when people run or sneak up on you suddenly? It may scare you when someone does that, right? Then a horse will feel the same way.

Shire

2-*Be gentle and talk gently to your horse*. There is no need to yell, shout or talk in a harsh tone to your horse. Again, this idea is not hard to understand. Do you like it when people talk to you gently? Or do you want them to shout and yell at you? Isn't it nicer to treat others kindly and don't you appreciate it when others do the same for you? Your horse will appreciate your kind manner too!

3-*Most horses love to be touched*. Show them your feelings through your hands. Stroke them on the head, massage their neck, hug them, brush them and communicate your affection through gentle fingers. Imagine how happy your horse will be!

4-*Try to spend as much time as you can with your horse*. In any friendship, regular visits are the key! No matter what you have to do, stop by and visit your horse just to remind them that you're there. They will be so happy to see you and the more you spend time with them, the stronger your bond will grow.

5- *A nice reward*. A tasty treat, rub or pat down, yummy food, grooming of whatever other treat you might have in mind, will be a great idea! Do this at the end of the day to let your horse know how much you enjoyed spending time with them.

Royalgrovestables.blogspot.com notes another beautiful attitude of horses. It is their intuition or intuitive nature. This means a horse can *sense* your feelings, emotions and will react on those feelings.

If you are angry, upset, unhappy or grouchy, the horse will sense these negative emotions. This will not help you to get close to them. Instead, they may avoid you. But if you are positive, upbeat and happy to be around them, they will feel this as well. This will draw them to you and you will be able to bond with them!

Chapter 2

Aren't my braids cute?

Have you learned anything new about Shires? Wonderful! But there is still more we can learn about them. And a great place to start is the Shire Horse Society. This charitable organization is dedicated to showing and preserving these amazing animals.

At Hurst Green in the UK, they have trained Shires for 13 years. They love it when people stop by every weekend to learn about riding and showing their horses. Have you ever heard about them?

Jacquie Gardiner at Hurst Green says: "*Shire horses are our passion and Hurst Green Shires is all about having fun.*"

Many different events are held and it is here that Shires really shine. And the nice thing about it is how much the horses really like it!

It is customary to see well groomed horses with their mane and tail braided with raffia in unique styles. Their owners and presenters are also dressed nicely. The idea is for everyone to look their Sunday best.

These amazing events celebrate Shires. The members who are part of this group and the Shire Horse Society are working very hard to save Shires for future generations!

Bonding moment

CURIOUS FACT FOR KIDS:

Horses, like us, have different titles for different stages of life. For example when a horse is born until 6 months of age it is called a *foal*.

Then up to the age of 2 years it is called a *yearling*. If the horse is a male horse it is called a *colt* under the age of 4. When it is older than 4 years it is called a *stallion*. Do you remember what a Stallion is?

Meaning of Terms:

A *stallion* is a: Male horse that can have kids.

A *gelding* is a: Male horse that cannot have kids. (Geldings are usually patient, calm, quiet and well behaved.)

A young female horse or pony is called *filly* and after the age of 4, she is called a *mare*. (Source: *Lessonpaths.com*)

Grass is yummy!

Shire

Chapter 3

There is no doubt Shires are unique horses. Here are a few additional facts about horses in general you may like to know. (Source: *Onekind.org*)

-A horse can express its emotions in many different ways. It can use its face, eyes and ears to tell you how it feels!

-Horses are great at keeping watch. It is rare to see a herd with everyone snoozing at one time. There is usually one horse standing as a lookout, and his job is to warn the others if danger comes near!

- Avoid standing behind a horse. They have great vision, but there are a couple of blind spots. Can you guess what the back part of the horse is? Yes! It's a blind spot. If the horse gets angry or scared, guess what he might do if you stand directly behind him?

-Horses are great at listening! They can turn their ears in different ways to improve their hearing. If you whisper and say something bad about your horse, they just might hear you!

- Horses can help people get better when they have mental or health problems. This is called: *Equine Assisted Therapy*.

Kay Baxter from *Ehow.co.uk* recommends the following for Shires:

Check the fence area and the stalls every day for any type of damage. Can you guess why? Do you remember how big a Shire is? What will happen if it leans on the door or gate too much? That's right! It might break, so you need to be sure that everything is locked up tight.

You also need to leave enough space so your horse can rest comfortably. Don't you like it when have space to move around, especially if you are resting? Your horse does too!

Fun to run in the snow

GENERAL HORSE TIPS FOR KIDS:

If you are able to get a horse, you will need to care for it. So here are some tips you can think about: (Source: Frank Bell-*Horsewhisperer.com*)

-Your horse's diet is very important. Some horses have very hot blood and some have cooler blood. If your horse is hot blooded, they will need less protein in their diet. Shires are cold blooded.

Shire

-Learn how to properly discipline your horse. Remember: These animals are very sensitive. Let them know when they are getting too out of control! This can be done with a shhhhh noise or a firm tone to let them know who is in control.

-If the horse's head is high it means your horse is not relaxed. They may be upset in some way. If their head if low they are relaxed. Try to get your horse to stay relaxed. This will help them feel good and both of you will enjoy the ride.

-Horses love to get your tender rubs and soft pats. Things like rubbing their ears, nose, eyes and mouth is great. And a massage is even better!

-If a horse is trained really well, he or she will invite YOU for a ride. You should be looking for the invitation! Then you will enjoy an awesome ride.

-Your horse can sense your moods and behavior. If you are confident your horse will be confident too!

-You should feed your horse from a bucket and not your hand. (This is the recommendation, but I feel it is better to feed them with your hand from time to time! It seems to generate more trust and respect, but that is just my humble opinion on the subject. What do you think?)

Enjoying the breeze

INTERESTING FACT FOR KIDS

Do you know the scientific name for horses? They are called Equines which comes from the Latin word meaning Equus Caballus. Can you think of any other creature that looks like a horse? Did you think of a donkey? Maybe a Zebra? What about a mule? These are also related to the Equus Caballus.

Horses can live for many years. Some for 30 years and in some cases 40 years or more! Ponies can live for a very long time too. But if you want to know how old they are you need to look into the horse's mouth! Have you heard of this practice before? Usually the approximate age of a horse is estimated based on the incisors, upper and lower in the mouth. What is that? The teeth!

Can you tell how old you are by looking at your teeth? (Source: *Lessonpaths.com*)

Conclusion

Fun to run!

In conclusion: Horses are beautiful creatures, and Shires are no exception. This patient, loving and strong horse is a wonderful example of how amazing Earth's creatures can be.

Shires are really neat. They are still faithful, loyal and willing to work hard. They are also happy to be a part of your life and with a little love and affection, your bond will grow.

This is a great time to learn a bit more about these noble animals. You may be amazed at what you can discover. If you don't know where to look, ask your teacher, a parent or guardian to help you. They may have some great ideas too!

If you don't know exactly what to research about this noble breed, then think about this: Why don't you choose something you really like (It can be the tail, mane, feathering, ears, body, size, personality, etc) and learn a bit more about that particular subject?

If you are in school and you participate in show and tell, use that as your subject. Many of your classmates may not even know what a Shire is, so it would be nice to share what you find with others!

I hope this book has taught you just how wonderful nature is and how each creature can impact our life in amazing ways.

Shires are truly one of nature's magnificent wonders!

Author Bio

K. Bennett loves to write for both children and adults. Many different subjects are interesting to develop, but writing for children is special to her heart.

Her favorite pastimes include reading, traveling and discovering new things. Each of these activities helps to fuel her imagination and acts like a blank canvas waiting for more stories.

She is intrigued with fantasy elements like hidden worlds and faraway lands. Basically anything that gets her imagination soaring to new heights!

Her writing credits include children books online, short stories for online magazines, and two novellas listed at Amazon.com

Our books are available at

1. Amazon.com

2. Barnes and Noble

3. Itunes

4. Kobo

5. Smashwords

6. Google Play Books

This book is published by

JD-Biz Corp

P O Box 374

Mendon, Utah 84325

http://www.jd-biz.com/

Read more books from John Davidson

Amazon.com Author Link

Shire

www.ingramcontent.com/pod-product-compliance
Lightning Source LLC
Chambersburg PA
CBHW050925290526
45792CB00002B/885